Practical Witchcraft

Magic Spells, Rituals, Potions and More

By Diana Abbott

Copyright 2015 By Crown Publications.

All Rights Reserved.

Witchcraft Defined

The term *witchcraft* evokes different images for different people. Many Westerners would be surprised to know that more and more of their contemporaries are embracing witchcraft as a viable expression of their own spirituality. However marginal or far out it may have seemed in the past, it is clear that witchcraft is becoming progressively more mainstream throughout the world.

Witches are people who revere both the God and the Goddess. They seek a more friendly relationship with their natural environment, endeavoring to recognize the sacredness of all of nature. Witches, further, seek to utilize cosmic or psychic forces to do their bidding. To this end, the practice of witchcraft involves knowledge and skill in appropriating the rituals that are believed to harness and focus these energies. Seeing themselves in stark contrast to other occult religions such as Satanism, witches seek to work these forces in order to enhance their own experience of life and to promote healing and community.

When one begins to investigate the phenomenon of modern witchcraft, it does not take long to notice a range of terms associated with the practice: *The Craft, Wicca, paganism,*

Neo-Paganism, and so on. Brooks Alexander, a researcher who is an expert on the occult and counterculture, gives a helpful summary of certain distinctions between the terms *Wicca, witchcraft,* and *Neo-Paganism. Neo-Paganism* is the broadest category, encompassing a wide range of groups "that try to reconstruct ancient, pre- and non-Christian religious systems—such as the Norse, Celtic, Greek, Roman, and Egyptian religions—as well as…various obscure, forgotten, and neglected occult teachings from around the world.

Witchcraft Is a Worldview. A worldview is the sum total of one's view of the nature of reality. Everyone has a worldview even if only a few reflect on their own. One's worldview encompasses one's views of how reality is composed, how it works, and how we as humans fit in or relate to our universe. It can entail one's views about the purpose of life and the origin and destiny of us all.

Naturalism. Starting at the broadest level and working down, it is fair to say that the worldview of witchcraft is naturalism. Naturalism is the view that there is no transcendent reality such as God that can intervene in the natural world. Naturalism maintains that all of reality is interrelated and operates according to "laws." Other expressions of naturalism would include materialism, which sees all of reality as being made up of matter that operates according to material laws.

Witchcraft, though an expression of naturalism, is not materialism. Witches recognize that reality extends beyond the realm of the material. This is sometimes confusing. A worldview can be naturalistic even if it accepts the reality of an immaterial realm; indeed, even acknowledging the existence of gods and goddesses does not preclude a worldview from being naturalistic. What stands in stark contrast to naturalism is a worldview that says that the natural realm (whether material, immaterial, or both) is the creation of a transcendent God. This is supernaturalism. This is what historic, orthodox Christianity is.

Occultism. Sharpening the focus, not only can we say that witchcraft is a worldview of naturalism, it is also a worldview of occultism. The term occult is from the Latin occultus meaning "hidden," or "secret." The category covers a wide range of beliefs and practices that are characterized by two main points that are often thought to be "hidden" from the average person. First, the occult maintains that there is force or energy into which one can tap or with which one can negotiate to do one's own bidding. The familiar term spell is applied to the technique of harnessing and focusing this power. The late witchcraft practitioner Scott Cunningham explains, "The spell is...simply a ritual in which various tools are purposefully used, the goal is fully stated (in words, pictures or within the mind), and energy is moved to bring about the needed result."6 Exactly what is the nature of this force or energy, according to the occultist, and what is the best way to work with it is what makes some of the main differences between the major occult groups such as shamanism, witchcraft, Satanism, New Age, and others.

Second, the occult maintains that human beings are divine. The practice of the occult arts is thus an endeavor to actualize one's own divinity. As witchcraft practitioner Margot Adler claims, "A spiritual path that is not stagnant ultimately leads one to the understanding of one's own divine nature. Thou art Goddess. Thou are God. Divinity is imminent in all Nature. It is as much within you as without."

Humanism. Witchcraft sees itself as a celebration of all life. This celebration involves the denial that there is anything wrong with the human race. The practicing witch Starhawk rejoices that "we can open new eyes and see that there is nothing to be saved from, no struggle of life against the universe, no God outside the world to be feared and obeyed"8 (emphasis in original). Pagan Elder Donald Frew of the Covenant of the Goddess explains, "How can we achieve salvation, then? We're not even trying to. We don't understand what there is to be saved from. The idea of salvation presupposes a Fall of some kind, a fundamental flaw in Creation as it exists today. Witches look at the world around us and see wonder, we see mystery."

Witchcraft Is a Practice. Notice that the term practice is often used with the term witchcraft. What this tells us is that, for many, Wicca is as much what someone does as it is what someone believes. While it is certainly true that what one does is invariably a product of what one believes, for witchcraft the emphasis is on what the practice can do to enhance one's own well-being as well as the well-being of others. Witches do not simply adhere to a list of dogmas; indeed, in many ways witches like to think that they eschew dogmas. As Adler describes it, "If you go far enough back, all our ancestors practiced religions that had neither creeds nor dogmas, neither prophets nor holy books. These religions were based on the celebrations of the seasonal cycles of nature. They were based on what people did, as opposed to what people believed. It is these polytheistic religions of imminence that are being revived and re-created by Neo-Pagans today."

A look through witchcraft material at the local bookstore will reveal that much of it deals with various rituals and activities that can be perfected in order to manipulate and utilize this cosmic or psychic force to do one's bidding. One will find chapters on the various items of clothing to wear (robes; jewelry; horned helmet, when one is not working naked, or "skyclad"); the tools to use (candles, herbs, tarot cards, talismans, fetishes); and rituals to perform (spells, incantations, chanting, music, dancing)— all of which enables the practitioner to become open to these forces (if they exist outside) or to conjure up these forces (if they originate from within). One will learn how to interpret dreams, meditate, have out-of-body experiences, speak with the dead, heal, and read auras. One can seek to develop one's own powers within the context of other witches (in a coven) or alone (in solitary practice). There are no obligations to follow any previously prescribed method. If what others have done before works, that is fine. If one sees the need to change the ritual or tools to get better results, then that is fine as well. All of these activities are designed to do two things: to enhance the well-being of one's self or those around him or her and to actualize one's own divinity.

Honey Love Spell

You will need the following items for this spell:

- A jar.

- Honey (Rose honey the best)

- Red paper.

- Green ink pen.

Write your lover's FULL NAME and BIRTH DATE on the red paper using green colored pen. Put it into the jar. Pour the honey into the jar, over the paper, until the jar is full.

Put the jar lid on tightly and leave it under your bed and DO NOT TOUCH it.

Stone Attraction Spell

You will need the following items for this spell:

- Any stone.

- Natural running water (stream, river, waterfall).

Take any stone. Hold it in your projective hand for several minutes while visualizing your need.

Flood the stone with your need and with your emotional involvement with your need. Send power out from your body to the stone. Use your visualization to see it streaming into the rock.

Then throw the stone into running water. It is done.

Sweet Jar Candle Spell

You will need the following items for this spell:

- Small, squat jar with a metal lid.

- Honey or molasses or maple syrup or corn syrup.

- Red pen or marker for love, yellow pen for friendship, green pen for business, etc. (check for colour magic).

- Piece of square paper (any size you want, but about 3"x3" should suffice.

- A votive candle in the colour that you require (red for love, green for employment, yellow for friendship, etc etc).

- A strand of the person's hair and a strand of your hair.

- Herbs relating to your need.

- A spoon.

Egg Bath Spell for Peace

You will need the following items for this spell:

- White candle.

- 3 eggs.

- White towel.

- White clothing.

- Birdseed or bread.

- A Tbsp. each of:

- Salt.

- Florida water.

- Rose petals.

- Mint.

- Parsley.

By the light of a white candle add the following to your bath:

Salt, Florida water, rose petals, mint, parsley, sage, bay leaf, rosemary, nutmeg and 3 eggs.

Bathe with the eggs, being careful not to break them. When you are finished, dry off with a white towel and put on white clothes.

Take the eggs to a wooded area or park and leave them under a tree along with birdseed or bread.

Exorcism Brew

You will need the following items for this spell:

- Rosemary.

- Bay.

- Cayenne.

- Water.

3 PARTS ROSEMARY.

1 PART BAY.

1 PINCH CAYENNE.

Mix, add one tsp mixture to a cup, pour boiling water over the herbs & let steep for 9 minutes, covered. Drink a few teaspoons a day, or add to the bath.

Home Cleansing Spell

You will need the following items for this spell:

- Sea salts

- Water

- Rose petals

- Sands

Add the sea salts, sands and rose petals into the water in a bowl. Wrap it with the black cloth for 3 days. On the third day, put the bowl outside. Leave the bowl outside for 3 days. On the third day, sprinkle the water around your house.

Astral Binding

You will need the following items for this spell:

- An understanding of meditation and sigil magic.

Meditate and leap to the astral level, find the victim who has wronged you. Place a circle around them, quickly construct this circle into a circular cage, with a roof on top.

Place onto the roof a sigil that you have beforehand made that will represent you, place magick into the sigil in some way (the astral sigil not the real one), any way is fine.

Now instruct the person that the cage is real and unbreakable and that they cannot escpace it unless you specifically let them out. Also instruct them that as long as they are in this cage, they must obey you completely.

Now do as you please. And enjoy your revenge. But be prepared, no one knows what might come of their actions, whether good or bad, this might help or hinder you, as any spell might.

To Freeze Someone

You will need the following items for this spell:

- Ziplock bag.

- Water.

- Freezer.

- Paper with the person's name or a photo of the person.

Put some water in the ziplock bag, close it, and put it in the freezer. Wait for the water to freeze.

Take the name of the person OR the photo of the person you wish to freeze and put it in the baggy, then fill with water until it's covered. Close the bag and put back in the freezer, and wait for the water to freeze.

If the paper/photo isn't fully covered in ice yet, add some more water, and freeze again.

Leave the baggy in the freezer. This will keep the person "on ice" throughout the time you have the baggy in the freezer.

Arthritis Healing Spell

You will need the following items for this spell:

- Powdered ginger.

- Few drops of Eucalyptus oil.

- Powdered allspice.

- Few sprigs of rosemary.

- Small bag.

Put all the ingredients into the bag and say:

"Bright blessings be on this bag today

may this spell take all pain and aches away

Let the energy of healing be in this bag so near

To heal and protect the one that I hold dear"

So Mote It Be.

Now visualise a bright blue light surrounding the bag and drawing into it. The blue light of healing.

Give the bag to the person that needs healing and they can either put it in a bath or keep it near them - especially in their bed at night.

Chakra Bath

You will need the following items for this spell:

- A tbsp of each:

- Red rose petals.

- Orange peel.

- German chamomile flowers.

- Slippery elm or blue tulip petals

- Lavender flowers.

- As well as:

- 1 clear quart.

- Handful of salt.

Run a bath. Combine all ingredients and put into bath with the water running. Ground and center in the tub. When soaking in the bath concentrate on each Chakra from the root up being fully opened cleansed and charged.

Career or Money Spell

You will need the following items for this spell:

- 4 tiger's eye crystals.

- 12 silver coins.

- Paper.

- Green pen or marker.

Place the four tiger's eye crystals in a square formation (East, West, North and South), leaving room for the silver coins to go between them.

Place 4 silver coins between each tiger's eye, creating a square. While you are doing this, picture yourself in that new job, or what you would do with that money.

Write on the piece of paper the job you want, or the amount you need and what you need it for, fold it up, and place it in the center of the square.

Now trace the square of tiger's eyes, starting in the East. As you trace it, see yourself working the job you want, or doing what you want to do with the money you have.

Say at each stone (in the proper Quarter):

Eastern beings see my request,

Bring to me what You think is best.

Northern beings hear my cry,

Bring this opportunity by.

Western beings know what I need,

And let me be the one to succeed.

Southern beings let good fortune come,

So I may have the proper sum.

Leave this small "altar" up, and perform the chant once a day until you receive what you require.

Third Eye Ritual

Perform this ritual three days before the full moon, preferably when the moon is in the sign of Cancer. Begin by brewing a strong tea made from yarrow or mugwort. Light thirteen purple votive candles to help attract psychic influence. Drink tea, stare into a magic mirror, crystal ball, or pyramid and chant three times:

"I invoke thee, O Asariel,

Archangel of Neptune

And Ruler of clairvoyant powers.

I ask thee now to open my Third eye,

And show me the hidden light.

Let me see the future.

Let me see the past.

Let me perceive the divine.

Kingdoms of the unknown.

Let me understand the wisdom

Of the mighty universe.

So mote it be!"

After chanting, relax, breathe slowly, concentrate on opening your third eye. Do not allow negative thoughts to enter.

Spirit Guide Spell

You will need the following items for this spell:

- A quiet place.

- Ability to visualize.

Relax your body.

Once you are completely relaxed, visualize yourself walking down a street. The street splits off into two paths: one to the forest, and one to the city. Take the path to the forest.

Enter it, and begin to notice the sensations of the forest. The liveliness, the flowers covering the grounds, the songs of the birds. Start to notice a large body of water to your right, and turn to it. Before it, lays a circle of stones. Enter the circle.

Once you have done this, you will feel peace. Bliss. You are happy. Close your eyes and bask in this warmth, and happiness. After a few minutes, you notice a shadow hovering over you. Open your eyes. When you are ready to see, you will see your spirit guide. Connect to them, get to know them.

At the end, thank your spirit guide for coming to visit you.

Contact the Deceased

You will need the following items for this spell:

- 3 white candles.

- A pendulum.

- A picture of the one you have lost.

Put the picture of the deceased on a table. Hold the pendulum above it. Around picture put the candles and light it.

Invite the deceased, you can say something like (Persons name) come at me,I want to speak with you. Use pendulum for speak with the deceased.

At the end thanks spirit for coming.

Sabbat Oil

You will need the following items for this spell:

- 3 parts Patchouli.

- 2 parts Musk.

- 1 part Carnation.

Wear to the Sabbats to promote communion with the deities.

War Water

You will need the following items for this spell:

- Cut nails.

- Water.

- Jar.

- Refrigerator.

Place cut nails into a jar and add water. Let them steep for a week or 2 until the nails have started to rust and add more water. Open jar occasionally so that fresh air will help the rusting process. Use when the water has a rusty tinge in it. Keep refrigerated.

For workings involving anger, conflict, protection and rage.

Honey Elixir

You will need the following items for this spell:

- Honey.

- Tea.

- Tea cup.

At noon on a Sunday, hold up honey to the sun that their double gold may run shining together, mixed as one. Add three spoons of honey to a cup of tea then say this:

Sun charge me,

Gold server me,

Alchemy change me,

Honey preserve me.

Witch's Bottle

You will need the following items for this spell:

- Glass jar.

- Your own urine.

- Vinegar.

- Rusty nails.

- Broken glass pieces.

- Broken mirror pieces.

- Your own blood.

- Graveyard dirt.

- Shovel.

- A place to bury the jar.

For protection of yourself, your home, and your loved ones.

1) Collect your urine into a disposable cup.

2) Gather other ingredients wherever you plan to do put the jar together.

3) Firstly, pour the urine into the jar.

4) Secondly, pour a cup of vinegar in the jar.

5) Thirdly, add a drop of your blood.

6) Fourthly, add the rest of the items (broken glass, broken mirror, rusty nails, graveyard dirt).

7) On a new moon dig a hole deep enough that the bottle will not be disturbed. Place the bottle in the hole and cover it up. Throughout this time, make sure no one sees you doing this, as that will make the Witch's Bottle unable to work. Bury near wherever you reside.

8) Leave the bottle for as long as you reside there. When you move, be sure to dig the bottle up, and smash it in a river or stream to undo the magic. Make a new one for the next place you live.

Consecrate an Object

You will need the following items for this spell:

- Incense (preferably Myrrh or Patchouli).

- 1 white candle.

- 1 bowl of water.

- 1 bowl of salt.

Take the item, cover it with salt, place your dominant hand over the bowl and envision a white light leaving your hand and passing through the bowl burning away all negative energies. Say:

"Blessed Lord and Lady, with salt and smoke I consecrate this tool in Your names. Let it serve me well."

Remove the item from the salt, shaking it off as you do so, then pass it through the incense smoke, sprinkle it with water, then pass it through the candle flame.

Meditation Tea

You will need the following items for this spell:

- 1 tbs. china black/english breakfast.

- 2 tsp. chamomile.

- 2 tsp. elder flower.

- 1 tsp. rose hips.

Boil fresh cold water in tea kettle; warm china/ceramic tea pot with hot water, pour out, add loose tea in china or ceramic pot; add boiling water over the leaves. Steep 3-5 minutes; pour tea through strainer into tea cup or strain into fresh, serve with milk, sweetener, lemon to taste. cover tea pot with cozy to keep tea warm; drink only 2-4 cups per day as tea in general acts as a diuretic and some herbs are not healthy in large doses. Add the herbs one by one stirring them.

Chalcedony Crystal

Energy: Receptive

Planet: Moon

Element: Water

Powers: Peace, Anti-Nightmare, Travel, Protection, Lactation, Luck Magickal Uses: Chalcedony, in common with many other stones, banishes fear, hysteria, depression, mental illness, and sadness. It also promotes calm and peaceful feelings when worn or held in the hand.

In the 16th century it was prescribed by magicians to dissolve illusions and fantasies. For this it was pierced and hung around the neck.

Worn to bed or placed beneath the pillow, chalcedony drives away nightmares, night visions and fears of the dark.

As a protective stone, chalcedony guards its bearer during times of political revolution and while traveling. It is also used to ward off psychic attack and negative magick. Chalcedony prevents accidents if worn.

In Renaissance magic the chalcedony was engraved with the figures of a man with his right hand upraised. This was worn for success in lawsuits as well as for health and safety.

The stone is used for beauty, strength, energy and success in all undertakings, and in Italy, mothers wear beats of white chalcedony to increase lactation. An arrowhead carved of chalcedony is worn and carried for luck.

Candle Blessing

You will need the following items for this spell:

- A White Unscented Candle.

- A Piece of Paper.

- A Pencil/Pen.

- A Match.

Light a white candle. Make sure it does not have any markings or other colors.

Write the names of the people you want to bless on the sheet of paper. Burn the paper completely and then blow the candle out.

Blessing Oil

You will need the following items for this spell:

- 1 tsp. lavender.

- 1/2 tsp. rosemary.

- 1 tsp. St. Johnswort.

- 2 drops juniper berry oil.

- 2 drops rose oil.

- 2 drops balsam or peru oil.

- 3 drops vetiver oil.

- 1/4 cup base oil.

Add ground herbs and drops of essential oils to base of spring water/oils: olive, sunflower, safflower, mineral; bottle with tight lid and store in dark place.

Luck Spell

You will need the following items for this spell:

- Small piece of ginger root.

- Fennel seed.

- Cloves.

- Dried basil.

- Small bag or pouch.

Put all the ingredients into the bag. If you have a small piece of any yellow crystal it is a good idea to add this too. Say:

"Herbs of the earth fill my life with light,

Bring me good luck in a day and a night.

This spell is steeped in magic and mystery,

Make my bad luck a thing of history.

Bad luck will go deep into the ground,

From now on good luck will follow me around."

So Mote It Be.

Keep the bag with you for a day and a night and then bury it deep in the ground - somewhere that is not on your property. This will bury your bad luck.

Witch's Garden

One does not follow the witches path long before feeling the need to garden. As witchcraft is an Earth religion, we feel a spiritual rush when sinking our hands into the soil or watching a plant grow to maturity. These are the energies we celebrate in our rituals, the handiwork of our Mother Gaia.

First and foremost, you must evaluate your magical needs. Use a lot of mugwort for divination? Constantly smudging the house with sage? These herbs would certainly have a place in your garden. Check out my Magical Uses of Herbs pages and find plants to meet your needs that are well suited to your area. Don't know which plants grow well in your area? Take a look at this planting zone chart for the US. Research this carefully.

Once you've chosen your plants, how is your magic garden different from grandma's mundane garden? Number one, you've chosen your herbs to match your magical intent. When grown, they will be blessed and charged in a magic circle to assist in your spellwork and ritual. But we can bless and charge our seeds and plants during the growing process as well, infusing them with magical energy.

Magically charge the water used to nourish your plants. This can be as simple as saying an incantation over the watering can or setting water out under the full moon to charge. Sprinkle a few fertility herbs or a moss agate in the water while charging. Again, draw fertility runes on your watering can and charge it with abundance.

Bless your plants with a mini-ritual every full moon during the growing season.

Healing Flames Spell

You will need the following items for this spell:

- 2 small pieces of paper.

- Pencil or pen.

- One red candle.

- A heat proof container.

- Match or lighter.

Draw a picture of yourself with the disease, wound or condition that will clearly point out the problem.

Charge the red candle with healing energy and light the candle. Hold the tip of your drawn picture in the flame.

After it is lit, drop it into the heat proof container and allow it to burn to ashes.

While the red candle is still burning draw another picture of yourself completely healed. Place this picture "below" the flame of the red candle and let the red candle burn out completely.

Tonic Wines

Tonic wine is a wine in which a single herb or blend of herbs, barks, roots or spices has been macerated for a short period of time. It is a pleasant and effective way of taking tonic & medicinal herbs to aid the digestion & strengthen the body. The most well-known and popular kind of tonic wine is the winter favourite mulled wine, a heated blend of red wine and orange juice infused with Cinnamon, Nutmeg & cloves. It is an excellent cure for the winter blues.

These are all suggestions to be added to a 750ml bottle of wine.

Borage: a handful of fresh herb steeped in medium white wine for several hours with the juice of a lemon makes a refreshing & restorative summer drink that lifts the spirits.

Cinnamon: one quill steeped in either red or white medium wine for one week, it sweetens the wine and is warming and stimulating.

Ginger: 1 piece of root steeped in red or white wine for one week. Ginger is revitalizing, warming and stimulating. Good for indigestion & colds.

Lemon Balm: a handful of fresh herb steeped in sweet white wine for several hours makes an uplifting & cheering wine, very good for the winter blues.

Peppermint: a handful of fresh herb steeped in a medium to sweet white wine is a good tonic wine, excellent for settling the stomach.

Sweet Woodruff: 5g of fresh flowering herbs steeped in medium white wine for 3 hours is an excellent tonic for strengthening the body and mind.

Rosemary: 1 bottle of medium white wine and 6 sprigs of fresh rosemary.

Witches Ladder

You will need the following items for this spell:

- About a yard of cord or ribbon in three colors - the colors depending on what you want to use the ladder for:

- Green for money.

- Red for passion.

- White for creativity.

- Black to stop bad habits.

- Brown for balance.

- Yellow for happiness.

- Orange for health.

- Blue for peace.

- Purple for wisdom.

- Beads, feathers or anything to knot into the ladder - the choice is yours. You will need nine of them.

Start the spell by braiding the three cords together, as you go you braid the beads, feathers etc into the ladder so you have nine evenly spaced items.

As you place each item in chant the following:

By knot of one, my spell's begun.

By knot of two, it will come true.

By knot of three, so mote it be.

By knot of four, this power I store.

By knot of five, my spell is alive.

By knot of six, the spell I fix.

By knot of seven, events I'll leaven.

By knot of eight, it will be fate.

By knot of nine, what is done is mine.

"The power has been raised and is now 'stored' in these knots, beads, feathers and in the cord."

You can tie the ends of the ladder together and use it as a necklace for protection on your person or hang it somewhere close to where it is needed such as your bedhead or chair.

If you want to use it for healing untie and release the items in the knots like this:

You must release the knots one at a time - one a day - for nine consecutive days. Release them in the same order in which they were tied. As the knots are released the energy that was put into them releases and is used for the purpose that the ladder was made for. You can either bury the beads etc, or keep them in a safe place.

Herbal Vinegars

Macerating herbs in vinegar is an excellent method of preserving their medicinal properties, as vinegar absorbs the minerals and calcium within herbs far more effectively than water does. Herbal vinegars are a good non-alcoholic alternative to tinctures, and an easy way to take tonic herbs. Externally, vinegar is antiseptic and anti-fungal. A cold compress will reduce swellings & ease sunburn as well as insect bites and wasp stings, but should never be applied neat, or on broken skin.

When making herbal vinegars ensure that all your equipment is clean and sterile. Do not use any metal implements when making herbal vinegars. Seal jars and bottles with glass stoppers or plastic lids, as metal and vinegar react badly with each other. If using fresh herbs, allow them to dry overnight in a cool, dark place, if damp herbs are put into vinegar, they may spoil.

Garlic: is antiseptic and antifungal, eases sore throats when gargled. It is also a good tonic that stimulates the immune system.

Chamomile: soothes itchy skin conditions. Added to bathwater it helps treat fungal infections. As a hair rinse, it soothes sore scalps & lightens hair.

Lavender: is antiseptic & stimulating. It makes a good hair rinse for dry and itchy scalps. It soothes inflamed or sore skin.

Peppermint: is antiseptic, making a good gargle for sore throats. It also eases sore gums & can be added to bath water to soothe sore skin.

Rosemary: is an excellent tonic herb. It is also good hair rinse for itchy scalps. It can be added to bathwater to soothe sore skin.

Sage: is antiseptic and a good tonic herb. Used as a gargle it soothes sore throats. As a cold compress it eases bruises. It can also be used as a hair rinse for itchy scalps, and to darken hair. Avoid use during pregnancy.

Thyme: is a powerful antiseptic & anti-fungal herb, it eases coughs & bronchial troubles. As a gargle it soothes sore throats & gums. Avoid during pregnancy.

Answer Spell

You will need the following items for this spell:

- Incense.

- A bottle.

- A seal.

- Wax.

Raise energy and once built up throw the energy into the bottle. Then Take bottle and sing the rhyme into the bottle, visualize the power of the words flowing into the bottle. Do this while outside and near the water, once done take a seal and place it over the top of the bottle, then pour wax around the seal. Keep bottle sealed as long as you want the spell to endure.

rhyme

Answers, answers, show yourselves to me,

Answers, answers, become visible for me,

Answers, answers, once this spell is done,

Answers, answers, your knowledge and mine will be one,

Answers, answers, this energy of mine as it be from me,

Answers, answers, blasts through the fog of ignorance,

Answers, answers, so that I may see you clearly.

So Mote It Be.

Revenge Hex

You will need the following items for this spell:

- Chicken bones.

- Hammer.

- Broom and dust pan.

- Cloth bag.

- Bell.

Gather bones of chickens and dry them in the sun for a few

days. Then when you are ready to do this hex make sure you

are worked up into a frenzy of anger and hatred. This will

add to the potency of your hex! Be thinking of all this

while doing this hex and when it says "With these bones I

now do crush," take a hammer or use your feet to stomp and

crush these bones as if they were your enemy before you!

When you are done sweep, them up and place them in a bag. You

will then want to sprinkle the dust and remains of the bones

on your enemy's property around his house.

If you have a bell ring it 3 times and say...

I call upon the Ancient Ones from the great abyss to do my

bidding I invoke Cuthalu, God of Anger and the creatures of

the underworld hear me now...

Bones of anger, bones to dust

full of fury, revenge is just

I scatter these bones, these bones of rage

take thine enemy, bring him pain

I see thine enemy before me now

I bind him, crush him, bring him down

With these bones I now do crush

Make thine enemy turn to dust

torment, fire, out of control

With this hex I curse your soul

So mote it be!

Protection Spell

You will need the following items for this spell:

- Visualization

Visualize a circle of bluish purple light forming around you and expanding into a sphere as you repeat this chant three times (each time form a new sphere).

Thrice round the circle's bound,

Evil sink into the ground.

Protect Against a Charm Spell

You will need the following items for this spell:

- 1 part myrrh.

- 1 part frankincense.

- 1 stone of jet.

- 1 cup of red wine.

Crumble myrrh and an equal portion of white frankincense into wine, and shave part of the stone Jet into the wine.

After fasting for a night dirnk this for three, four, nine or twelve mornings.

Rain Spell

Chant this:

Mother Water

Heal My Thirst

I Grow Weak

Mother Water

Heal My Thirst

Quench My Pain

Bring The Rain

Mother Water

Heal My Thirst

So Mote It Be!

Seasonal Rain Spell

You will need the following items for this spell:

- Rice.

Spread the rice around the area you wish it to rain and chant the following:

On these places that there is rice

some seasonal rain would be nice

but not so much the rain should flood

or those in need would drown in mud

Anu and Lou blessed be

and as my will so mote it be!

Snow Protection Spell

You will need the following items for this spell:

- One peppercorn.

- A pinch of salt.

- Pinch of powdered ginger.

- Pinch of powdered cloves.

- A small piece of red cotton cloth.

- A bowl.

- Needle and thread.

Place the peppercorn in you bowl saying and visualizing:

I charge you with protection.

Place the salt in saying: I charge you with stability.

Place the cayenne pepper in saying: I charge you with warmth.

Place the ginger in saying: I charge you with protection.

Place the cloves in saying: I charge you with protection.

Mix the assembled spices and salt with your fingers, visualize yourself having a safe health, guarded time. Now transfer the herbs to the center of the cloth squares. Fold in half and in half again and sew up the ends. Carry this with you. Make a new charm ever snowy season.

Forgiveness Spell

You will need the following items for this spell:

- Bunch parsley.

- Bowl of water.

- White ribbon.

Tie the ribbon round the parsley bunch. Dip the parsley in water and then sprinkle the water over yourself using the bunch of parsley. While you do this chant:

I wash away all hurt and pain,

I wash away deep wounds like rain,

All shame and guilt depart,

Let deep forgiveness heal my heart.

Hang the parsley over your bed while you sleep. In the morning bury it along with all your pain.

Fire Scrying

You will need the following items for this spell:

- A candle which must has connection with your question (for example a red candle for a love question).

- A quiet, dark room.

Find some place comfortable and begin to relax yourself, however method you prefer. Clear your mind, and focus on the question you wish to ask. Light your candle. Focus on the flame, focus on your question. Images should start to appear, such as: if you question is about school, you will see an image of a book. Some images will personally mean something to you, and you will know the answer.

Truth Spell

Picture the face of the person you want to tell the truth.

Chant:

Shadow of lies, fly away, and let the truth shine and stay.

Moon Candle Spell

You will need the following items for this spell:

- Large sharp tree thorn.

- White candle.

- Fire.

- Occult oil.

On Luna's Day, after She is new Cast off anything that may be blue. To work this spell in Monday's power Do this at the Midnight Hour.

Take a large and sharp tree thorn and a short white candle with the Waxing Moon adorn, by pricking and sticking its shaft so pale the symbol that the Moon Goddess doth hail.

Then dress this lamp with an occult oil damp.

Light the wick with intention thick and concentrate your wish most firm, as the flame begins to sputter and squirm.

Chant this then thrice that it may suffice:

QUEEN OF HEAVEN, STAR OF THE SEA,

FILL MY CUP WITH PROSPERITY.

SILVERY GODDESS ENTHRONED ABOVE,

FILL MY LIFE WITH ABUNDANT LOVE.

BLESSED GODDESS, SO MOTE IT BE!

68200700R00027

Made in the USA
Lexington, KY
04 October 2017